How To Be a Mentor for a Day

Planning for the Day
Planting for a Lifetime
(Second Edition)

by
Craig Thompson

Published by Thompson Publishers

The Mentoring Revolution Series: Book One

Thompson Publishers
https://thompsonpublishers.com

How To Be a Mentor for a Day: Planning for the Day, Planting for the Future (Second Edition)
The Mentoring Revolution Series: Book One
Copyright © 2019 by Craig Thompson

Requests for information should be addressed to:
Thompson Publishers, PO Box 2605, Cleveland TN 37320-2605

ISBN: 978-1-64407-008-6 [softcover]
ISBN: 978-1-64407-009-3 [ebook]

All rights reserved. No part of this book may be reproduced, stored in a retrieval system, or transmitted in any form or by any means -- electronic, mechanical, photocopy, recording, or any other -- except for brief quotations printed in reviews, without the permission of the publisher.

Scripture taken from the New King James Version®. Copyright © 1982 by Thomas Nelson. Used by permission. All rights reserved.

Cover photo courtesy of Petra Thompson © 2017.
Cover design Craig Thompson © 2019.

Printed in the USA.

"With the ancient is wisdom;
and in length of days understanding."
Job 12:12

Other Books by the Same Author

The Mentoring Revolution Series
52 Godly Mentors Parent's Planning Guide

Asking for Wisdom: Maximizing Your Time with Mentors
This book is written for youth and is intended to teach them how to ask the kinds of question which will provide them with wisdom for living.

Nurturing Your Children Through Mentors
This book gives parents an understanding of the numerous ways a child can benefit from meeting with mentors. Examples from the lives of children who have met with mentors are included in each chapter.

The Mentoring Revolution Small Group Curriculum

Stories for Children
John and Gayle Stories

Other Works
Preaching Through Proverbs: A Collection of Sermons by the Pastors of Central Africa

Contents

Foreword
Our Story 1
How to Use This Book 3
Congratulations! 5
What Is a Mentor? 8
Why Mentors? 13
The Impact of One Day 16
The Key Word 21
Why Me? 25
Preparing for the Day 31
Asking Questions 43
Personal, Legal and Ethical Concerns 52
Go and Do Likewise 57
Examples of Mentoring 61
Acknowledgments 86
About the Author 87
Comments 88
Errata 89

Foreword

I was sitting by the pool with other parents of our youth group one Sunday evening during the summer of 2017 as a group of middle school students from our church were milling about. Some were swimming, others were eating pizza, while others were out in the yard playing games. As parents of three students, my wife and I enjoy opening up our home for youth to come over and hang out. We value the life, energy, and community that it provides. However, I had also been wanting to find a way that my wife and I could pass on some spiritual lessons to our kids and some of their peers in a small group setting. As Craig and I talked, he told me about a mentoring program that he had developed for his kids where they would meet with a mentor every week over the course of a year. At the time, he was developing a curriculum for churches and small groups. This immediately grabbed my interest, as I had been influenced positively by mentors throughout my life. It sounded like a great way not only to help my kids but others as well.

We decided to move forward with the curriculum and involve our boys in the pilot program. Over the course of the next school year, we started meeting with a group of 7-8 boys, including our own, on Monday nights. We would have a different mentor from our local church come and speak. The men were from all walks of life: pastors, missionaries, educators, an insurance salesman, a lawyer, etc. They shared their testimony, spiritual lessons, and what it meant to be a Christian in their particular field. After the first few months, I found myself writing notes down from the weekly sessions when I would get home. I remember thinking that I wished that I had heard such wisdom when I was a teenager!

The group rotated mainly between meeting at Craig's house and ours. This was beneficial in a few ways. When we met at the Thompson home, I had a good uninterrupted 15-minute drive back to my house where I could discuss things further with my son. However, by meeting at our house, my wife was able to overhear some of the mentors. She thought it would be terrific for our daughters, so she and a few other moms organized a girl's group that began meeting at our house.

As the school year ended, my son asked if we were going to do the same thing the following year because he enjoyed hearing the different speakers. When I asked him what he felt like he learned the most, he said it was learning how to stay 'God-focused' while being successful in life. We started meeting the next year with a different format which was focused on the spiritual disciplines, and I continued to see positive growth in my son's life. It was no longer just his parents and youth pastor telling him biblical principles; now he was hearing from other people each week testifying of God's work in their lives and the change it made. During one of the mentoring sessions, we made notecards with a list of items the Bible says to pray for. It was encouraging to see that notecard on his night stand for months after as he continued to use it to pray for those requests.

Mid-way through the second year, my wife and I accepted a position with our church ministering to the middle school youth. We had seen such a positive response in our family as well as other families in the mentoring program that we wanted to find a way to implement this in a church setting. Currently, we are setting aside one Sunday evening a month for our middle school youth to split up between the girls and boys and have a mentor for both groups come and speak. We are fully on board with this style of mentoring and see in it a great model for intergenerational ministry to fulfill Psalm 145:4 which says, "One generation shall praise thy works to another, and shall declare thy mighty acts."

I am excited that Craig is writing this book, and I encourage you to consider these principles to see how you can positively influence the next generation.

Eric Whitaker, Middle School Pastor
Westmore Church of God

1
Our Story

It was 3 a.m. on a cold night, and I was sick. I'm usually healthy, but something had gotten the best of me. As a result, I was sleeping a lot, and my sleep schedule was completely awry. If it's the middle of the night and I can't sleep, my general rule is to do something profitable. That could be praying, reading the Bible or working on projects. This night, I was praying and meditating. I was also thinking about my son's upcoming birthday.

For a couple of years, I had been thinking of what I wanted to do for his thirteenth birthday. I had been thinking about having him meet with different businessmen, entrepreneurs and leaders each week for a year in order to help mentor him and shape his development. The problem was that I could not get any peace. Something kept nagging at me that the idea was incomplete.

So, at 3 a.m., wide awake and wrapped in a blanket, I was sitting in my living room with no noise or distractions. In the stillness of that moment, as I was reflecting on my plans and trying to sort through why it didn't feel completely right, it was if God dropped into my mind the missing piece: 52 GODLY men. When that occurred, everything became crystal clear. I had been focusing on men with successful business qualities rather than on men of character. My son needed to meet with men who may not seem to be successful in the world's eyes but who are successful in the broader scope of life, family, and relationships.

It was as if a veil had been removed from my eyes. I retrieved a pen and a piece of paper and began to write furiously as the names of godly men I knew began to come to my mind, men of integrity, men of solid character, men who are willing to take a stand for what is right in the face of great opposition, men who had endured conflict and suffering but who had come out the other side better and not bitter. I think I probably wrote down over thirty names in just a few short minutes.

The rest is history — and a lot of hard work. My son met with a different man each week over the course of his fourteenth year. That year was a rite of passage for him from childhood into adulthood. His character was challenged and sharpened, his personality strengthened and refined, his worldview enhanced, and his knowledge of life was broadened through the weekly sessions with the different men.

Since that year, I've had two daughters meet with 52 women each, and my second son is about halfway through his program. This has been a life changing journey for each of them.

From the beginning, I always felt in my heart that this concept was not just intended to be for my family alone. Rather, I believe that it is a framework which can be used by families everywhere to the benefit of not just their children but also our communities and nations. This book is one of many steps I am taking to help make our next generation stronger and better. But the heart of this program is the many mentors who are willing to share their time and their lives in order to impact youth. Thank you for what you do!

2
How to Use This Book

When I first began 52 Godly Men, I did not have a book which I could hand to the men who would be meeting with my son and say, "Please read this. It will help you as you prepare for the day you spend together." After sending three children through the program, that need has become even more apparent. Quite simply, we don't have good training in our society on how to be mentors. Most people have never had any training. While I believe that the men and women who have met with my children have done a good job with them, the feedback I have received from some of them is that they wish they had a better idea or plan on how to prepare for the day.

While I hope that people read this book through from cover to cover (at least eventually), I realize that some people are looking for quick ideas. Because of that, I have made the chapter titles very descriptive. Further, each chapter has a summary at the end which lists the key points for that chapter. These paragraphs are highlighted with the heading "**Key Points**." Feel free to scan through each chapter and read the key points. This is particularly useful if you need to get ideas for one or more areas in particular or if you want to beef up on ways in which you can impact a young life.

There are several chapters which will guide you through making a list of names. For these, you can use paper and pen or a note on your mobile device. Primarily, you should use whichever type of format is most helpful to you in your daily life.

If you have any questions on something which is not clear, or if you have suggestions on how to improve this book, please contact via the online contact form at https://walkwithgod.com. Your input can help us to make this a better resource for the person who could be mentoring your own child or grandchild one day.

3
Congratulations!

First of all, congratulations on being asked to be a mentor for a day. Any time a parent or guardian asks someone to spend time as a mentor with his child, it is an honor. Children are our most precious trust as parents. (They're not really our possessions because they end up leaving us.) For a parent to ask you to serve as a mentor means that you have qualities in your character or life which are admirable. The parent wants you to share some of who you are and what has made you successful in order to hopefully make an impact on the boy or girl with whom you spend time.

In picking mentors for my own children, I can assure you that not everyone has agreed wholeheartedly with me that he or she could be a good mentor. Some people just don't appreciate the value of their own lives. I know people who have taken a stand on key truths in their lives. They have held onto their beliefs through thick and thin. They have suffered the fires of adversity and come out the other side stronger and purer. Yet, some of these people don't think they have anything to teach my children! I see lessons of patience, endurance, commitment and understanding of true familial and marital love. They look through their own lenses of self-doubt, struggles, trials and scars from decisions gone awry.

So, if you are currently feeling a bit confused as to why someone would ask you to spend time with a child, don't spend too much time on figuring it out. Just realize that someone else values your life and character. Accept it as a big compliment. Then spend your time working through how to make the biggest positive impact you can in the time you have to spend as a mentor.

For those who are comfortable in their own skin and realize that they have lessons from life to share with the next generation, you may simply need to think through what is the most important thing you want to share with the child you meet. Gifted teachers can sometimes overload others with more information than they can process. This book will attempt to help you in narrowing the lessons you have learned to appropriate bite-sized amounts which can be ingested by the young person with whom you are meeting.

Above all, unless you know for certain that you should not be a mentor for some reason, then please contact the parent or guardian and tell him you accept. Sometimes I have had to work through potential mentors being in a period of sickness or recovery, and some mentors really do have extremely busy schedules. As a parent, I'm willing to schedule months in advance or wait a year in order to have certain mentors fit my child into their busy schedules or to recover from a bout of sickness. I would simply encourage you to always lean toward the answer "yes" when someone asks you if you would be willing to impact a young life for good.

A final note: don't tell someone "no" simply because you don't believe you know how to be a good mentor. That's why I wrote this book! By reading this book, you will pick up enough key points that you can have a very rewarding experience mentoring a young person — so much so that I believe you will want to do it again.

Key Points

- Being asked to be a mentor is an honor.

- Don't overthink the opportunity. Instead, realize someone values your character and life.

- Unless you have a compelling reason not to impact a young life for good with what you have learned, go for it.

- Don't be afraid of what you do not know about being a mentor. Instead, read this book and learn how to have a great mentoring experience.

4
What Is a Mentor?

For many people, their biggest concern will be that they have no idea what a mentor is or how to be a mentor. This is because in Western society, we haven't had very many recognized mentoring relationship structures. Most people have heard of mentors or mentoring; they just don't have a clear picture of what it is. Let's look at what a mentor is and explore a few examples.

What is a mentor? My definition of a mentor is this:

> "a person who intentionally spends time with another person in order to help shape his character, skills or understanding."

Let's unpack that a bit at a time. The first part says that a mentor is a person. It doesn't say what kind of person. There are no restrictions on age, ethnicity, race, gender, socioeconomic status, religion or even health. When I ask people to mentor my own children, I want to find a diverse group of men or women. The point is, don't disqualify yourself mentally because you don't think you measure up to other people. One of the mentors I asked to meet with my son many years ago was a man who had little money and never went beyond a high school education; but he was one of the meekest and humblest men I've known. I wanted him to spend time with my son because of his character, not because of any of the other things with which he might be tempted to compare himself with other men.

The second part talks about intentionality. We'll talk about that more in a later chapter. For now, realize that if Dad or Mom had not asked you to spend time with a child, and if you had not said "yes" to the request, this would not even be happening. Someone had to make a decision for the mentoring to occur.

Next, the definition says that a mentor "spends time with" another person. This is vital. One of the greatest mentors who lived is Jesus of Nazareth. While He preached to thousands, He had an inner circle of people with whom He spent time day in and day out for several years. The heart of mentoring is being willing to share your time. *You are being asked to take someone else into your own inner circle for a period of time.* When this happens, a person is exposed to lessons and new relationships which he may never have been privy to otherwise.

The next part of the definition says "another person." It's necessary to look at this because we live in a world in which robotics and artificial intelligence are actually being touted as replacements for relationships with living, breathing human beings. Without dwelling on this too much or arguing the basic limitations of artificial intelligence, only human beings are equipped by design to explore the wonders of the universe together in relationship. This is done in marital relationships, the nuclear family, the extended family, communities, business and also mentoring relationships.

The last part of the definition informs us that there is a purpose for a mentoring relationship. That purpose is to help shape the character, skills or understanding of the other person. Some of this can happen just in the process of spending time together. However, the degree to which this happens will often depend on your determination and preparation as well as the interest and abilities of the person you meet with. You control only half of the equation, but it's a crucial half. It's a possibility that you may end up spending time with a child who really isn't interested in your profession or skillset. That doesn't mean you can't teach her something about business, marriage, raising children, making good decisions or any number of other important life lessons. However, you may end up spending time with a youth with the mind like a steel trap, an IQ near 200, and a hunger to learn like a dry sponge. In such a case, your determination to share, that inner choice which says, "I'm willing to be vulnerable and share some of my own hard-earned lessons" will be the decisive factor in making the most impact on that child.

Now that we have looked at the definition of what a mentor is, let's review some examples. As we have already mentioned, Jesus of Nazareth mentored His twelve disciples. In reality, there was a group of people which numbered more than twelve which followed Him around. Jesus was willing to let His disciples watch Him throughout the course of a day. They ate together, slept in the same place, walked together, rode in boats together, and dealt with the normal course of human existence together for a little over three years. Apart from the supernatural aspect of His life, the teaching method Jesus employed made a lasting impact on His followers. The leaders of the Jewish religious community made a point of stating that they realized "that they had been with Jesus" (Acts 4:13). It was time spent together over a long period of time that shaped the character, skills and understanding of His followers.

In ancient history, the Greek philosopher Socrates was a mentor to Plato. Plato then took what he had learned and mentored Aristotle. Aristotle himself mentored a young man named Alexander who conquered the known world by the age of 25. History also shows us through the role of the apprentice and master craftsman how mentoring relationships can be lived out. In recent times, Sally Ride became the first woman to travel into space. She credits Dr. Arthur Walker, her graduate school professor, as being a mentor who believed in her and encouraged her to apply to NASA's space program. Steve Jobs, the late founder of Apple, served as a mentor to Mark Zuckerberg, the head of Facebook. Like them or not, both men developed companies and products which have had a global impact. Tom Brady, winner of four Super Bowl championships (out of eight appearances), fifteen division titles and numerous other awards, has been mentored by his coach Bill Belichick, a coach known for taking good players and making them part of a great team.

Each of these relationships involved a mentor helping someone to become better at a skill or to grow in understanding about life, business or a craft while spending time with them. These people were impacted by the mentor's belief in their ability to succeed. As a final note, we will use the word "mentee" to reference the person who is being mentored. This can be a child, a youth or even a person already in a career or who has begun a family. The mentee is the person you are meeting with in order to mentor.

Key Points

- A mentor is a person who intentionally spends time with another person in order to help shape his character, skills or understanding.

- Many people throughout history have been urged onto success because a mentor was willing to teach them and provide a critical element of believing in their abilities. Simply put, mentoring is one of the best ways to impact current or future generations.

- You can be a mentor if you are willing to share your time, open up your life a bit and relate the lessons you have learned in your successes or failures.

- A mentee is a person who is being mentored.

5
Why Mentors?

With the resurgence of mentoring, there can be hype and a level of excitement which surrounds the topic without people really grasping its importance. Is it important? Why should we mentor or have mentors in our lives?

My wife and I have been married a long time, yet we still seek out mentors for our children. The reason for this is simple: we are imperfect and imbalanced people. We come at life from a set of experiences which have helped to shape us, but it doesn't mean we understand everything there is to know about life. By seeking people to help mentor our children, we are both acknowledging that we cannot teach our children everything they need to know about life or about specialized topics, and we are inviting other men and women to share their expertise in order to round out the education of our children.

If we find mentoring a necessity in a family where both father and mother are present, how much more is this needed in our society where, due to the breakdown of marriages and the nuclear family in recent generations, the rise of single parent homes has increased dramatically? Children in the West are growing up without the influence of a father or mother. Whether through death, arrest, divorce or misguided priorities, the children of our communities are being robbed of the role models they need throughout the critical stages of their growth. This lack of role models in the immediate home life has negative consequences which can be lifelong. At-risk children need to see men and women of character living out their daily lives in order to begin to have a glimpse of how different life can be from the pits or ruts of bad decision making and shortsightedness that they see in their own families.

By saying "yes" to an opportunity to mentor someone, or by actually taking it upon yourself to seek out a youth to mentor, you are helping to give at least some light of hope to a life which may have little to none. Mentors can help to break cycles of negative thought patterns. They can point a child in a different direction or open up a door of opportunity which never would have been available otherwise.

In the classical example of a master craftsman and an apprentice, the youth might be apprenticed to a tailor, a carpenter, a printer or some other tradesman. He would spend long days watching the craftsman at work and doing whatever was requested of him. Whether it was running around the community getting supplies or delivering orders, he simply did it. Parents impressed on the youth that this was an opportunity to learn a real trade which would give him a chance to start his own business and make money as he grew up. People did this because it worked. Spending time with a master of a trade eventually rubbed off on the apprentice. The youth's own willingness to learn and attention to detail played into the equation, certainly, but in those days there were few safety nets of governmental assistance. You worked, or you went hungry.

Governmental intrusion into the social order has done

much to destroy the will to succeed. Yet, today, there are still plenty of young men and women who are eager to learn, want to grow, and are in need of men and women who will help guide them along the path of growth and maturity. The need is increasing for good mentors to step up and provide direction.

Key Points

- The destruction of the nuclear family has created a tremendous need for male and female role models.

- Even children raised in a healthy, traditional two-parent home benefit from exposure to mentors who can balance their education in ways the parents are unable to provide.

6
The Impact of One Day

At the writing of this book, three of my children have been through a 52-week mentoring program which I initiated for them (52 Godly Men and 52 Godly Women). A fourth child has been a part of a nine-month mentoring pilot program for churches and small groups and is about to begin his 52 Godly Men experience. Because of my commitment to this, I have gotten to see firsthand what can happen in a child's life as a result of his or her experiences with a mentor. Here are just a few of the things which have occurred in their days with men and women they met.

One of my daughters, Anna, had an absolutely irreplaceable experience with one of the women she met. After spending a day with this woman, she discovered that she never, ever wanted to have a job like hers. The woman herself was friendly and likable, but the job stretched the limits of the definition of boredom for Anna. While that may seem like a strange experience to relate as the first example of what can happen in one day, I list it because it's a very valuable lesson. I went to college with people who spent four years working on a degree which, when they entered the real job scenario, discovered they really didn't like the job for which they had been training. Those people spent possibly $100,000 only to discover what my daughter learned for free in one day just by spending time with someone doing the job.

The same thing occurred when we had a foreign exchange student stay with us. She wanted to become a midwife. We knew a midwife, and I asked her to let our guest spend a day with her. After spending one day with the local midwife, she realized that she really didn't want to do that job. When she went home, she focused her studies elsewhere. I counted that as one of the big successes of her time with us.

My son, David, spent time with an editor at a local newspaper. While he knew that he was pretty good with writing and grammar, he had never really thought about using those skills in a job. When he spent a shift at the newspaper, he saw what a real editor does, and he even got to edit a few articles himself. (That was all fun and games until he started finding errors which the staff had missed.) That day with the editor wasn't counted as his "Top Five" experiences when he was 13 years old, but now that he is an adult and has majored in journalism, he counts that day as a formative experience in his life.

Both of my daughters who have been through 52 Godly Women have met with women who have done some type of cooking with them. Anna met with a woman who showed her how to bake a cherry pie. They spent time preparing the base and the filling and then worked on the lattice pattern for the top crust. Petra met with one woman who made several different types of desserts and allowed Petra to help and learn. Probably the highlight of cooking experiences for Petra was meeting with a woman who runs her own bakery. They spent the day talking, laughing and decorating cakes. Petra worked with materials and ingredients she had not been exposed to previously, and she had a fun-filled day in the process.

Earlier, I mentioned that being a mentor involves opening up your inner circle with another person. This has been repeated over and over with people who have mentored my children. David met with a Christian lawyer who was serving as legal counsel with local government at the time. He introduced David to the mayor and other local leaders. Petra met with a woman who operates a booth at a trade show. She introduced her to the man who spearheads and is in charge of the entire event. The same lady, when she met with Anna, took her to a day-long event for women and introduced Anna to the speakers when they shared a table at lunch.

One of the men who met with David taught him about gun safety and the basics of hunting. Then he took him out hunting. David had a successful hunting experience and took another step forward in his development as a man by proudly and literally putting meat on the table.

Anna met with a counselor who has spent a lifetime helping people work through problems. During their time together, she talked with Anna about keys to dealing with harmful or negative thought patterns. Rather than waiting until she encountered problems, Anna had a tool in her arsenal to recognize and deal with negative thinking before it became a problem because she met with this woman.

One of the men I asked David to meet with was in an intercultural marriage. While I didn't anticipate that my son necessarily was going to seek such a marriage, I wanted him to hear about this man's experiences. By talking with him about the many challenges that one faces when bringing two entirely different cultures together in the context of marriage and family, it allowed David to see that having a good marriage involves much more than simply "finding a good woman."

Many of the men and women who have met with my children have taught them tips about marriage or raising children. One of the best life tips I witnessed was in the pilot mentoring program we had for middle school boys in which my son Paul participated. A local lawyer from our church was talking about how he had broken off a relationship with a young woman who would have been the dream woman for many young men. She was rich, educated and beautiful. When pressed on why he had broken off that relationship and started a relationship with the woman who is now his wife, he gave a very practical but seldom voiced answer. He said, "I couldn't picture myself raising a family with the first young lady, but I could see myself raising a family with the woman I asked to be my wife." What an incredible life tip for evaluating future relationships for these young men. This jewel of truth came out during a 90-minute evening session in a small group.

These are only a few real-life examples of how my children have been influenced by men and women who were willing to spend just a small amount of time with them. It's worthwhile to remember that my children would not have even had these experiences if a parent had not sought out mentors for them and asked men and women to be willing to spend time with them. And they certainly would not have had the chance to meet these people and learn these lessons if the men and women had not been generous enough to say "yes" to the request. I also want to point out that none of these were mentors who met with my children over the course of days, weeks or months. These were all examples of the impact a mentor can have in a single day.

Key Points

- Mentors can share nuggets of truth or teach a skill all within the time frame of one meeting.

7
The Key Word

In some of my other books, I address the topic of the role of parents in seeking out mentors for their children. This is an intentional choice which parents must make because most people are not seeking out youth to mentor. However, there is also a need for the mentors to be intentional if the mentoring experience is to be successful.

Being intentional in mentoring is more than showing up and letting someone watch you go about your day. It means that you understand that there are lessons you have learned in your life which you can and should pass along to the next generation. You must evaluate your toolbox of life lessons and pick out the ones which you think need to be shared with the mentee.

This involves a bit of thinking on your part. What are the hallmarks of your life? What are the issues which are most important to you? If you were asked to give a speech on any topic to a graduating class, what would you choose as your topic? Have you encountered great adversity in life through poverty and hardship but managed to overcome it? Do you know how to start businesses? Do you know how to raise balanced and respectful children? Can you operate woodworking equipment with your eyes closed? Can you explain mathematical concepts and equations so that a child can grasp them? Is your passion ending the blight of human trafficking or the killing of the unborn? Do you desperately want people to understand that there are children who go to bed hungry in most communities in the world? Have you suffered through the loss of a spouse or a child and learned to work through grief to return to a life of joy? Are you known as a really good cook and love to share generational recipes with young people?

Let's use that last example and describe various scenarios. Picture in your mind a grandmotherly type who is going to fix something to eat for a guest. If the guest is a young woman, she may pull out her fine china and have tea with some sweets in a cozy setting somewhere in her house or on the porch. If the guest is an older couple coming over in winter, she might reach into her cookbook and pull out a favorite soup or stew recipe. If the guests are a young couple from the community, she might fill the table with meat, vegetables, fresh bread and a delicious pie. If the guest is a grandchild, however, she might instead make a big pot of macaroni and cheese. The chef and hostess is intentional about what she fixes for each type of guest based on the culinary knowledge she possesses and some presumptions she has to make about their desires. She also wants to serve what is fitting based on the weather and any other external factors.

Sharing knowledge is very similar. A mentee who is a preteen or just hitting puberty is going to have different questions, issues and interests than a student who is about to graduate high school to either begin a career or head to higher education. A mentee who is already in higher education will have a different set of needs and questions. If you have an opportunity to mentor younger children, the wonder and fascination they show toward learning all sorts of knowledge makes them a veritable sponge. If your mentee is a person in his late 20s or 30s, his questions will be completely different from most of the others. Your job is to reach into the cookbook, or storehouse, of your life and find the right set of ingredients for a good mentoring experience.

Some lessons are too complex for a young mind without the ability to break them down into bite-sized pieces. Talking about microscopic cellular biology in order to discuss the role of mitochondria could require several discussions in order to clearly present the information. Some lessons may not be age appropriate for the mentee. Discussing the intimate details of human reproduction and childbirth may not be the best topic for a ten-year-old child. Some lessons may not be suitable because the mentee has no foundation for them. Imagine a theologian wanting to discuss the finer points of the Book of Revelation with a mentee who was not raised in a home which espouses a belief in God.

This doesn't mean that you cannot — or should not — introduce advanced concepts to a mentee. Indeed, this is one of the roles of mentors: to introduce the mentee to topics, thoughts and issues they would ordinarily never encounter. However, the lessons themselves need to fit the mentee as best as possible. The best mentor in history, Jesus of Nazareth, dealt with the people who listened to Him this way. Mark 4:33 says that Jesus spoke to the people who listened "as they were able to hear." He was dealing with men, women, youth and children of many different backgrounds and educational levels. He knew how to simplify grand principles for audiences ranging from a couple of dozen to several thousand. He did not overwhelm them with information which they simply were not able to receive or process. Instead, He gave them lessons and stories which were best suited for that audience at that time.

Key Points

- Being intentional in mentoring means that you analyze your own life to determine which key lessons you believe you should share with the mentee.

- Being intentional means evaluating the mentee in order to determine how much information he is able to process out of all that you have to share.

- Make decisions about what lessons from your life you want to share and what parts of those lessons are age appropriate.

- You can introduce issues, topics and areas of knowledge which are completely new to the mentee, but you should take care to focus on helping the mentee understand what you share.

8
Why Me?

If you are recognized as a teacher or a leader, live a strongly self-aware life, are comfortable in your own skin 24x7 and have either benefitted from mentoring relationships or have served as a mentor to several people, you can probably skip this chapter. If, however, you are brand new to mentoring and really didn't have any significant mentoring relationships as you grew up, you should read on. This chapter is for the people who really want to know, "Why me? Why little old me? What could I possibly say or do with a young man or young woman which will really help them to take a step higher in their own lives?"

Having been through multiple years of education, including several levels of higher education, I can state from my own experience that most people who have been through higher education generally have been taught very little about introspection. It doesn't mean that most people don't do it. It just means that the business of life prevents many people from really practicing a routine and frequent critical analysis of their own journey through life. The concept of a journey is a good picture of our lives. It's a journey in which we meet new fellow travelers. We learn about the paths which seem to be easy but turn out to be dead ends. Some people turn around and head back to what they know is the main path, and others stay stuck in a dead end. We pick up tools along the way which help us on our journey. We explore relationships with fellow travelers, some of which are helpful and some of which are harmful to our progress. We stumble blindly at times due to a lack of knowledge or our own indecision. We make stupid choices. Occasionally, though, whether by careful thought or what may seem to be chance, we make right choices which turn out to be gold mines. Sometimes we focus on the gold excessively to the exclusion of our relationships and then later decide, correctly, that the gold itself is only a tool on our journey. Some people believe that the whole journey is a comic play while others firmly hold to the belief that there is a God who is guiding them through it all. Ultimately, we all must accept the fact that our journey begins with birth, and we experience growth as we live our lives. We begin to experience the decay of age, and finally, we all must face death and the end of our journey here on this Earth.

What about you? Where are you in your journey? If you are to share poignant lessons with the next generation, you must evaluate your own path in order to recognize the decisions and choices which led you to where you currently are. In this chapter, we will look at a few tools which can help you to discover just what "little old you" have to offer a young mentee.

First, before you strain your brain trying to exercise self-reflection, use your relationships to help you get started. If you have a spouse, a mentor, a lifelong friend, a coworker who knows you pretty well, an aged parent, a sibling or a pastor, set aside a time in which you go to these people and read the following statement and questions. (You should write down their answers either during the time you spend with them or immediately afterwards.)

I have been asked to spend time with a (young man/young woman) in order to mentor (him/her) for a day. I am wanting to be intentional about my time with (him/her) in order to make a positive impact on (his/her) life. I would really appreciate your help in evaluating my own life to determine what my strengths are in order to decide what to share with this (young man/young woman).

1. What is one positive character trait which you think I best exemplify?

2. Why did you choose that trait?

3. What is the greatest challenge or obstacle you have seen me overcome?

4. What do you see as one or two of my greatest passions or causes that I consider important?

5. Based on what you know about me, what are some of the skills I know which I could teach or unveil to someone in a day, even if it's just at a basic level?

6. If I were spending time with your child, grandchild, niece or nephew, is there anything in particular you would want me to do with him or her? This could be something fun, something serious, something spiritual, something educational or something business-oriented.

7. When I meet with the mentee, what story from my life would you most encourage me to share?

8. Based on what you know about my relationships, what is the best lesson or truth I could share with a mentee about relationships?

9. Based on what you know about my finances or business acumen, what is the best lesson or truth I could share with a mentee about financial decision making?

10. Based on what you know about my spiritual journey, what is the best lesson or truth I could share with a mentee about how to grow or develop spiritually?

11. What do you consider the area I need to work on the most in order to be balanced in my own life?

That last question may present more of an "ouch" moment for you, but if you are to make the most of your time with a mentee, it could involve being transparent about your own greatest challenge at this particular moment. Although some of these questions may make you feel good about yourself, they are, for the most part, seeking practical information which you can use to evaluate your life. If the people who give you answers know you intimately or have been around you for a long time, you need to set aside your emotions and open-mindedly look at the answers they give to you, whether you like their answers or think they are completely inaccurate (and occasionally they may be). This is the way the people who know you the most see you best, so their answers at least bear consideration and serious pondering on your part.

When you have gotten answers to these questions from a few of the people who know you, then you should compare the notes you made of their answers. It shouldn't be surprising if several of the answers are the same or similar. Nor should it be a surprise if some of the answers are totally different. After all, each of the people have known you for different lengths of time, on different levels of intimacy and have watched you at different parts of your journey. In reading through and thinking about their answers, you should place them on a scale. If several people stated that your best character trait is your patience, then think about how you developed that trait — or how life developed it in you. If you get vastly different answers about what you can teach someone else, then spend some time thinking about which one you would really like to teach or which you think would fit the best with your mentee. Keep your notes from these questions and answers. You will need them as we begin preparation for the time you spend with the mentee.

The point of this exercise is to help you discover, perhaps for the first time, what your contribution really is to the human race, your family and those around you. While your greatest tests or contributions may lie ahead of you, your time with the mentee should be based upon who you are today, how you understand your journey, and what you are willing and able to share from that journey.

Key Points

- Self-reflection is important in order to determine what parts of your life you should share as you prepare for your time with a mentee.

- Asking for feedback from those closest to you or who have known you a long time can provide you with a perspective on your strengths and of the topics which you are best able to teach to someone else.

- Using the questions listed in this chapter is highly recommended.

- Write down notes from the answers you receive to use as you begin to prepare for the day you spend with your mentee.

9
Preparing for the Day

This chapter follows a different format from the previous ones. As you read the chapter, it will guide you through a checklist of ideas and steps. It follows a logical flowchart progression and includes lists as well as thoughts and ideas on how to make the most of the day through the preparation you do. Let's get started.

The Top of the List
One of the questions I have posed to some of the mentors who have met with my children is this: If my child were going on an ark of some kind which was limited to a very few people, what is it that you believe is the most important skill, truth, technology or any other thing which you believe you should pass on to my child. That can help people to distill the very important from the ethereal. This could include a book which you believe every young person should read. If so, buy a copy and present it to the mentee. It could be teaching them the age-old patterns of sowing and reaping, planting and harvesting of seeds and crops. If so, plan to teach that. Whatever that most important thing is, make sure it is at the top of your list.

Whatever your passion is, consider making that part of your list if it already isn't at the top. Some of the men and women who met with my children were passionate about a cause, and their passion actually helped ignite interest in my own children simply because of the fervor these people exuded. If you strongly care about an issue, then be willing to share that with your mentee. You could be the only person with whom they ever meet who cares about the issue as much as you do.

Plan Your Talking Points

Take the notes from your self-reflection and the answers you received from your family and friends and look through them. Ask yourself which parts of your life you think would best fit this particular mentee. Make a short list of the following items:

- top three stories I want to share from my life, in order of importance

- top skill I want to share or demonstrate

- secondary life lessons or skills to share as time permits

- the primary character trait which others recognize or admire in me

- key spiritual truths, life lessons, financial wisdom or similar knowledge you have gained which you know how to teach

- areas of life in which you are currently growing or struggling

These are your rough talking points. You need to sort them by order of importance. It will help if you make a list on paper or on your mobile device to which you can refer. Meetings with a mentee can be hectic, but usually they are at least dynamic. It's easy to forget something which you consider important in the busyness of the day. You can add to the list as the day approaches or rearrange topics as you see fit.

After you set your list of talking points, check them to see if you need any photos, documents, or resources/supplies related to what you want to talk about. Photos (or diagrams) are still worth a thousand words, especially if you are sharing a personal story or technical information.

Have Activities Planned for Hands-on Lessons
Write down the top activities you want to accomplish with the mentee. This might include things such as demonstrating how to operate a lathe, hiking up a local mountain, showing how to prepare a PowerPoint presentation for a business meeting, baking a cherry pie from scratch, or any number of other activities you consider important.

Write down secondary activities you want to accomplish if you have extra time.

Look at your list of top activities. Determine if there are any permissions or forms which must be filled out to do any of the activities. This might include notifying an employer of a job shadow, getting a parent to sign a waiver allowing a ride along in a patrol car, getting copies of insurance details for a site visit or other similar paperwork. Start the process of getting the paperwork in hand to the appropriate parties and follow through with getting it filled out and ready.

Review the list of top activities and determine if you need to procure any supplies or facilities in order to have them available on the day of the meeting. Do you need ingredients for baking which you thought were in your cupboard but really are not? Do you need to secure a conference room with a projector? Is the equipment you wish to demonstrate to the mentee in working order? Is the hiking trail closed due to a government shutdown or a local park service maintenance issue? Check everything you will use. Downtime is wasted time. Take care of the details on the supplies or facilities you will need.

As you get closer to the meeting day, don't forget to check the weather. If your activities include outdoor locations, you may need to reschedule or choose alternate activities. Don't wait until the day of the meeting only to find out that everyone else in your region is hunkered down for inclement weather.

Secondary Activities

Take your list of secondary activities, the ones you want to include if you have enough time, and list them in order by ease of inclusion or your own preference or the availability of facilities/resources. Let's take the idea of a mentor wanting to teach a mentee about local flora. You might wish to make a hike in the woods your main activity, but if you have time, you might include related or unrelated activities such as

- a swim at a local pool or popular swimming hole to relax

- a visit to an ice cream shop to talk and reflect on the day

- a stop by the forestry office to look at their museum of leaves, nuts, bark, and items related to your main lesson

- a visit to a local cabinet shop which uses some of the local woods you talked about in their products

In the above list, the swimming hole may be near the hiking location, and the ice cream shop might be on the way to the forestry office. However, if you think that the forestry office has the best museum of local flora samples in the country, that probably should be at the top of the list.

Consider the previous list's items about permission, checking for the availability of a location or its operating hours (when does the forestry office close each day?), and whether you need to take any supplies with you to have available at a particular location.

The Parable of the Jar

In time management training, the story goes that a speaker stood in front of an audience. In front of him on the table, he placed an empty, very large glass jar. He asked the audience if the jar was full. A few people responded, "No."

The speaker picked up a box from under the table and took out several very large rocks. He placed as many of them as he could into the jar. When the pile inside the jar was near the top, he asked, "Is the jar full now?" Several people in the audience said, "Yes. It's full."

Then the speaker reached under the table and pulled out another box. From this, he withdrew a canister of gravel which he proceeded to pour into the jar filling the space around the big rocks. He looked at the audience and asked, "Is the jar full?" The audience gave mixed responses. Some said, "Yes" while others said, "No."

The speaker reached under the table and pulled out another box. From it, he pulled a bag of sand which he poured into the jar. The sand filtered down into the jar in and around both the large rocks and the gravel. He poured until the sand was level with the top of the jar. Having done that, the speaker asked the members of the audience, "How about now? Is the jar full?" The audience almost in unison shouted, "NO!"

Reaching under the table one last time, the speaker pulled out a large container of water. Carefully, he poured into the middle of the jar mouth. The water began to find all the empty space which was left. He poured and poured until the water was running over the top of the jar onto the table. He placed the water container on the table and asked, "Is the jar full now?" The audience shouted, "Yes!"

Looking at the audience, the speaker said, "What does this example teach us about time management?" One person raised his hand and said, "No matter how busy you think your schedule is, you can always find time to fit in something else." After hearing the response, the speaker paused and then said, "You are absolutely wrong." Pointing to the jar he said, "The lesson about time management that this jar shows is that if you want to fit the big rocks into the jar, they must go in first. Otherwise, you will never fit them in. In time management, you must learn to prioritize and put the important matters first on your schedule. There will always be other distractions, responsibilities or demands on your time which will easily and quickly fill up your day. If you don't work on the important things first, you'll never find the time to get them done."

So, as you plan for your meeting with your mentee, determine what the big rocks are. Focus primarily on scheduling them, preparing for them and setting up your meeting location in order to make sure that you talk about the most important topics or do the most important activity. If you do this, the chances of the meeting being successful will be immeasurably higher.

Meals

Some of the most relaxing and unguarded times in human relationships happen over meals. Thus has it ever been. People have to eat, and they typically use it as a time to relax. If you are able to spend time with your mentee over one or more meals, I highly recommend it. It will be a natural time in which to talk about some of your stories or life lessons you wish to share.

Determine your location. This could be your home, a company break room, a fast food restaurant, a fine dining establishment or a park bench. Whatever you pick, consider whether or not the location is conducive to private conversations where you both can feel at ease sharing personal details or life stories. If you pick a restaurant with obnoxiously loud music or where the booths are packed so tightly you can hear your neighbor's heartbeat, that may hinder conversation. If you pick a park bench but you meet in Winter, your mentee may be a cold-natured person who is more interested in getting warm than listening to you talk.

Either ahead of time or the day of your meeting, find out if your mentee has any particular food allergies. When I was a child, this wasn't an issue. Today, it's a reality that more and more people are facing. If there are no issues, you have a broader set of choices.

If you can meet for breakfast, that can be a good way to spend time getting to know the mentee before starting the day's activities. In particular, you can learn a bit more about her social skills, education and intelligence level, interest in the meeting and other factors which could affect what you share and how deeply you go into any particular topic.

If breakfast isn't available or if you are meeting at a different time frame, lunch can serve as a good break to what you have been doing. It can serve as a question and answer time where you get feedback from the mentee on what they have been learning and if they are enjoying their time.

If you are able to have a final meal at suppertime or a snack at a coffee shop or ice cream parlor, such a time can be a great way to put a lid on the day. The work is done, the activities are accomplished (hopefully!), the stories have been shared, the lessons passed along. You can use the time to get to know the mentee better, share additional stories or just enjoy your time together.

Have a Plan B
While most of this chapter is about developing a plan, it is also important to have a Plan B in case things just don't go according to plan. Stuff happens. Weather changes unexpectedly at times. Business emergencies happen. Unexpected closures of key locations could affect your plans. What will you do? Switch to Plan B — if you have one. The main points behind developing a Plan B are as follows:

Ask yourself what you would like to do if none of your primary activities are available. You should have a list of secondary activities and topics. Keep those on a list or in your mind.

Be flexible. If you planned to fly kites, and the expected winds died down, don't let it ruin your day. Your mentee doesn't have to know ahead of time what you are planning to do unless there were permission forms and such paperwork which were completed ahead of time. If you exhibit flexibility, then the mentee can learn that important life lesson from you.

Realize that the mentee can learn as much about real life from watching you deal with plans which get broken as he could going through the previously planned day. Broken plans are part of life. Maybe your contribution to his life is to help him see how to deal with disappointment gracefully and how to make the most of an unexpected situation.

If your plans do change, be sure to stay in contact with the mentee's parents or guardians so they don't end up wondering where their child is. If you move from Plan A, which is job shadowing you at your office to Plan B, which is rock climbing a 100-foot cliff, then you should certainly clear that with the parent before making that type of switch. Exercise common sense.

Corporate Considerations and Job Shadowing
Other than the aforementioned issues with getting the appropriate permission to have a mentee accompany you to work or shadow you on your job, there are a few other thoughts to consider. These are listed below.

Notify your coworkers. Some of them may have jobs which you would like to share with the mentee. Knowing this ahead of time allows them the courtesy of doing their own preparation. Other coworkers may politely decline, and you can avoid unnecessary tension by putting them on the spot the day of the meeting.

You should address any matters of corporate data security.

For instance, if you work in a medical setting, allowing someone to job shadow you could require having him sit in a chair where he cannot see a computer monitor where private patient information is displayed. Alternately, you don't want to be working at soft drink manufacturer A and have your employer or boss find out that you are mentoring for the day the daughter of the president of soft drink manufacturer B. Think through conflicts as much as possible.

Is there any particular attire the mentee needs to wear at your workplace? Steel-toed shoes? Slacks instead of a skirt? Skirt instead of jeans? No shorts? No open-toed shoes? A jacket because your office is freezing? Pass this information along well in advance.

Consider having a company owner or member of management give a five-minute speech on what your company does and what makes it a great place to work. You never know. The mentee could be your next employee — or your next boss. (I was once in a position of helping to make a decision about whether to hire a former boss of mine.) Plus, the chance to talk about their company can help management to better appreciate and buy into the mentoring process in which you are engaged.

If possible, give a brief company tour and describe to the best of your ability what each section does and how it fits into the whole. Your company may have a standard tour which someone from HR gives.

Whether your job involves sitting at a computer most of the day or operating a piece of machinery, take time to talk about the details of what you are doing and why they are important. You have probably forgotten most of the tiny details which were so hard for you to remember at the start of your employment. Dredge those out of your memory and go over them. Why does a fraction of an inch matter on your machine? What is a lockout procedure, and why is it important to human safety? Who has the right to shut down a production line? Who knows? What you share may help your mentee make a decision that she never wants to do your job, which would save her years of college debt getting trained for something which doesn't fit her personality. Or, the reverse may happen, and the mentee may realize this is her dream job, which causes her to double down on schoolwork.

In summary, this chapter has guided you through several lists and questions to help you develop your Plan A and your Plan B for the day you spend with your mentee. It is not meant to be exhaustive and comprehensive of everything you need to think of, but it should at least serve as a solid guide for getting you on the right path. In conclusion, I would encourage you to say a prayer asking for guidance from God on how to plan. Then remember that Proverbs 16:9 teaches us that a man makes plans in his mind, but the LORD directs his steps. Be flexible.

Key Points

- Read this chapter.

- Plan primary activities.

- Determine backup or secondary activities.

- Choose your talking points.

- Plan for meals.

- Take care of any job shadowing requirements ahead of time.

- Have a Plan B—be flexible.

- Keep focused on what the big rocks are, and put them into the jar first.

10
Asking Questions

In my book for mentees entitled *Asking for Wisdom*, I devote a fair amount of it to teaching them how to ask the right questions of mentors. In their time spent with a mentor, one of the most significant ways they can find out information to help them to grow in their lives is to ask the right question at the right time to the right person. But the reverse is also as important if not more important.

Mentors need to ask questions which will cause the mentees to think long and hard about the direction they are headed. They need to learn to ask the probing questions which cause discomfort and leverage the forces of change in their mentees. But as with mentees, many mentors have never developed a good repertoire of questions.

In this chapter, we are going to look at questions which mentors can use to prod, direct or challenge their mentees. Instead of coming up with my own list, I reached out to over a thousand people who have either participated in the program, heard about it, or have followed my children as they journeyed through their own mentoring experiences. I asked them to share questions which they have been asked throughout their lives or, maybe more importantly, what questions do they wish someone had asked them when they were younger. The responses were really insightful. As you read them, you may wish to write down some of them or variations of them to ask your mentee.

What questions do you think mentors should ask their mentees?

What is the most important choice you can make in life and why? (Rita Carrion)

My biggest question for a young person to consider is, "Do you know you have the ability to choose?" This is a question that can go a lot of different ways. My main point is that when a challenging circumstance comes your way (such as getting picked last for the team or having the popular girl in school say something mean to or about you), know that you have the ability to choose your response. You don't have to suddenly react with anger or shame. Those are natural responses and easy to wander into, but you don't have to go there. You are not trapped in only this option. Yes, some situations are downright ugly. A huge revelation to me was knowing that I was capable of responding well. Maybe it was just walking away from the situation, carefully thinking about what is really true, or going to ask someone for help. When I found that out — that grace is what allows you to respond rather than react—that was pivotal for me. (Merrily Suits)

What do you feel is your calling in life? What are the three top goals for your life? (Anita Hughes)

What would you do differently if you could live your life again? How would you define your relationship with God? Who is God to you? How would you like to improve your relationship with God? (Embry Milo)

Do you love Jesus? Do you truly love him? If not, is it because you don't know His character or who He is well enough? How do you love God more? (Karen Whitaker)

I was asked by one of our strong church members if I loved my hair more than Jesus. (Ed McGee)

The most important question to ask a young person is, "What do you think is the most important 'thing' that you could be, should be, or will be committed to in your lifetime?" Following are several quotes which I think could help a young person answer this for themselves. (Dave Whitaker)

> My Pledge - America must win this war. Therefore I will work, I will save, I will sacrifice, I will endure. I will fight cheerfully and do my utmost, as if the issue of the whole struggle depended on me alone. (written on the flyleaf of a diary found on the body of Martin Treptow, a World War I soldier)
>
> Great? Do you think that greatness just hatches like Malvy's canaries? Someday you'll learn that greatness is only the seizing of opportunity, clutching it with your bare hands until the knuckles show white! (Mi Taylor – the character played by Mickey Rooney in the 1944 movie, National Velvet)
>
> Be brave, be strong and do it. (King David's dying words to his son, Solomon, specifically concerning the building of the Temple in Jerusalem; 1 Chronicles 28:20)
>
> Be strong and of good courage, ...being careful to do according to all the law which Moses my servant commanded you; turn not from it to the

right hand or to the left, that you may have good success wherever you go. (Joshua 1:6-7)

Courage is being scared to death, but saddling up anyway. (John Wayne)

Most great men and women are not perfectly rounded in their personalities, but are instead people whose one driving enthusiasm is so great it makes their faults seem insignificant. (Charles A. Cerami)

Opportunity is missed by most people because it is dressed in overalls and looks like work. (Thomas Edison)

Do you really know what you are thinking and feeling? So many times we are not honest with ourselves about where we really are concerning the issues at hand. Because of this, there can be an unintended duplicity, weakness, or compromise hidden within our "godly" responses and reactions to the things around us. One of the reasons that we do not face off with the question of "Where am I, really, with this issue/situation/person?" is that we are afraid to stare our sin and flesh in the face for what it is. But God already knows what is there. He will meet us where we really are, not where we wish we were. (Michael Gravitt)

Are you feeling alone? (Queen Jones)

God what do you want me to do with my life? How do you want me to pursue your plan for my life? (Richard Snyder)

In your time with God and His word, what are some of the things that He highlights or brings to your attention? When you sense God speaking to you, what are some of the things you hear Him saying? What does that mean to you? (Iris Ray)

Do you know any person you would like to be like when you are an adult? What do you admire about them? What kind of person would you like to marry? Why? Is there a person you dislike? What do you dislike about him/her? Do you think you have the same traits sometime? Do you believe God has a plan/purpose for your life? How can you find it? (Naomi Thompson)

What questions do you wish mentors or leaders had asked you when you were younger?
I have a great question I wish someone had asked me when I was a pre-teen: "What would this look like if it were easy?" The question takes the focus away from working hard and puts it on working smart, which leads to success. Many people try to do their work with excellence but end up overcomplicating the situation, project, book or program they are creating. As a result, the project, program, book, etc. languishes for years or never gets finished because it's too hard, too complicated, too confusing. The next time you find yourself struggling to get started, to get something done or to get a project finished, just ask yourself that one question. Then wait for an answer to appear. (Karen Brunet)

Where are you in your relationship to Christ? Are you doing your part to enhance that relationship? What does that look like? Who do you presently look up to and for what reasons do you think so highly of this person? How much time have you spent in conversation with your parents this week not talking about yourself but talking about them? Whose life are you investing in besides your own? I've heard it said, "We are the sum of the five people we're around the most." What kind of person does that make you? (Gayle Cobb)

Timing

When to ask questions is just as important as asking them at all. In general, meal times often present the best opportunities for deep conversation and reflection. If you are having breakfast with a mentee you've never met, that time might best be spent just asking questions related to getting to know the person. If you know him, however, then the same time could be spent asking more serious life questions in order to set the tone for the day and future conversation. If you have just spent a day together sharing about your job or a skill, then a dinner together might be the time to ask questions related to career.

Often, the mentors who met with my children would have a time in which they would just sit and talk with them about their own lives and journeys. By opening up and simply sharing about what they had done, where they had gone, their struggles and successes, it then gave them an opportunity to ask questions. Having such a time with your mentee is a good idea. After you open up about your own life, ask questions to find out what their thoughts are about your journey. The sheer fact that you are transparent and are willing to engage in some self-reflection can teach your mentee what it means to truly think long and hard about one's own path.

After asking a question of your mentee, listen to her. Realize that she may never have been asked so profound a question. She may stumble over her answer. But knowing that you are listening and that you really are interested in her answer can empower her to push through the discomfort and newness and begin to actually examine her own choices, motives and thought processes.

Be willing to ask follow-up questions. The classic follow-up questions are "Why?" and "How?". But you can use any follow-up question to dig a bit deeper. Here are a few examples:

- What career would you like to have when you are my age? What type of preparation or training do you need in order to be in that career? What steps are you currently taking to make that happen?

- I noticed that you were short or curt in your answers with your Mom when she dropped you off for this meeting. Why is that? How is your character being shaped daily by the way you have chosen to respond to your parents?

- How much money do you have saved up right now? What percentage of the money you receive do you put aside into savings?

These types of questions are designed to go somewhere. You can use a well-ordered series of questions to help a mentee arrive at more than just an answer. A series of questions can help him to arrive at a destination, a place of discovery or revelation.

Normally, a mentor will use many questions in a question-and-answer format to engage a mentee in dialog. However, a really good mentor knows that there is a time and a place after asking a question where he should be willing to let the question stand. Not all questions are meant to be answered immediately. Some take a lifetime to answer. Some require experiencing a bit more of the twists and turns of life before a person is able to face up to the question.

When I met with a young man recently as part of his mentoring program, I asked him several pointed and personal questions. He told me that he really appreciated me doing that because it helped him to open up about his own thoughts on issues he faces in his life. He also confided that he only has one or two peers his age with whom he feels that he can open up to about the questions he has. This gave me the opening to tell him that I am available for him to talk to whenever he wants to in the future.

I heard a story one time of someone who was invited to interview for a job which he really wanted. The CEO of the company reviewed his resume and educational experience. Afterwards, he looked the applicant in the eye and asked him pointedly, "When you were in college, did you do your best in your classes and your assignments?" The applicant was unnerved by the question and had to answer, "No. I didn't." After another pause, the CEO ask him, "Why not?" Then the CEO turned around in his chair and ended the interview.

While you or I cannot guarantee that such a compelling question will result in a change of behavior on the part of the mentee, we can plant the seed and hope that it will fall on good ground and yield fruit. That is your role as the mentor; and it is worth noting that some questions, like some seeds, are designed to grow slowly and produce fruit years down the road.

Key Points

- Mentors need to use questions to help mentees think about the consequences of their choices and the direction they are headed.

- You can read the lists of questions for good examples.

- Develop your own set of questions which should include questions you wish someone had asked you when you were younger (or questions someone did ask you which helped you).

- Look for the right time to ask a question. Do not force a question just to ask a question.

- Some questions deserve an immediate answer, and some questions are long term questions which are designed to make the mentee think for weeks, months or even years.

11
Personal, Legal and Ethical Concerns

Thousands of years ago, Solomon wrote that a prudent man sees danger coming and protects or hides himself, but the foolish barge ahead and end up in a mess (my loose translation). In today's world, we have to face the reality that, at least in Western cultures, we live in a litigious society. People sue, accuse, point the finger and sometimes go into a situation knowing that that is what they are aiming for. Police have conducted stings to catch such hucksters in the act, but human nature and the overabundance of lawyers willing to accept what could often be frivolous lawsuits have brought us to where we are today.

What a way to start a chapter in a book on mentoring, right? But if you are to have a good day mentoring a youth, you need to have an understanding of what may be wise ground rules or even add some of your own. In this chapter, we will look at a few of the issues you may wish to consider when being a mentor for a day. This chapter is not intended to be an exhaustive list nor should it be construed as legal advice. Rather, I'm simply trying to offer some wisdom based on my own life experiences and what I have observed in the lives of others. If you want legal advice, consult an attorney.

Determine your policy about accepting opposite gender mentees. With my children, the boys have all met with men, and the girls have met with women. That is simply due to the fact that I'm trying to develop character in them which is commensurate with their own gender. While I believe that men can teach girls good lessons and vice versa for women and boys, for my children, I am focussing on them learning from their own gender in order to help them to clarify their own personality, skills and abilities.

If you have no issues with mentoring someone of the opposite gender, you should still set up some guidelines which allow the interaction to take place without ever putting yourself in a position of someone being able to accuse you falsely. It happens. Good ideas include meeting in a public place, making sure coworkers are always around, not meeting behind closed doors or in a secluded area of a workplace, and not driving alone with the mentee.

Even if you only meet with mentees of the same gender, you still might wish to adhere to some of these ideas. Unfortunately, my generation saw an explosion in the number of reported cases of child abuse from same-sex offenders. Wisdom simply reminds us to try to look out for the potential of harm, whether through false accusations from a parent or the smearing of our name via innuendos from coworkers.

Determine your policy about being in a vehicle alone with the mentee. Many of the mentors who have met with my children have driven them somewhere, whether to a park to talk, a forest to hike or to a restaurant to eat. However, one of the men who met with my first son would not take him to or from lunch. I had to pick up my son, drive him to the restaurant and then back to the man's office again. Who was he? He was a state representative. He explained it simply: "I make it a policy not to be alone in a car with a minor who isn't my own child." Period. Given the issues surrounding politicians, I think that was wise for him.

Record your interaction. Some states or countries allow one individual in a conversation to record his interaction with other individuals without having to notify that they are being recorded. Not all states or countries allow this. You should check your own laws. Most places do allow you to record a conversation as long as both parties are aware of the recording. You can record as easily as using an app on a cell phone or other mobile device. Or, you can revert to the standalone digital recorders typically used for voice dictation. While a recording could interfere with the dynamics of your interaction with a mentee, chances are it also quickly will be forgotten, allowing you to conduct your conversation with a natural flow.

Reserve the right to end a mentoring day at your discretion. Some men are simply uncomfortable being in the presence of a teenage girl who is dressed very scantily. Some women do not want to be around a teenage boy who is high on his own testosterone and gives off the air of someone looking for a conquest. It is more likely than not that you will not have one of these experiences. But you have the right to make it clear that you can and will end the mentoring day if lines are crossed or even approached too closely for your liking.

Determine your policy about touch. I live in a touchy part of our country. Men and women routinely give hugs or display affection in groups when they are entering or leaving church, homes or even business functions. Not everyone is comfortable with that. When in doubt, stick with a firm business handshake. While human touch has its important place in relational and emotional human development, mentoring for a day may not be one of those places. Of course, there are some grandmotherly types who will read this and say, "I'm going to hug that girl or boy anyway." I understand that mentality. If you hug everyone you meet and are known as that, then that is part of who you are and what you bring to the table as a mentor. As with all of these pointers, exercise wisdom.

Determine your policy about gifts, donations or charity. Several mentors have shared gifts with my children. They like that. I am fine with it. It teaches the basic concepts of sharing and receiving which we want our children to learn. Books are the most common gifts my children have received. A book you have written, signed by you, or a book which greatly impacted your life makes a great gift. You also may meet with a mentee who comes from a poor or even destitute background. Do you give charity? Do you buy her some clothes? That decision is up to you. Again, it may make the most impact to hear your story and then receive a dress and pair of shoes which allow your mentee to look fit for an office. After hearing you talk about a particular craft or skill and seeing you demonstrate your abilities, the life changing moment might come when you give your mentee a tool you no longer need or have replaced with a newer one. It is also possible that a gift of money or something else would cloud the relationship. The greatest gift of your time, good advice and a clear set of steps on how the mentee can improve his lot in life could be the impetus he needs to step up and earn his own money.

Make it clear whether or not you will provide a meal for the mentee. While I highly recommend meals as a great time to relax and talk, mentors are not always flush with cash themselves. If you cannot afford to take your mentee to a restaurant for a meal, let the mentee or the parent know that clearly ahead of time. However, you should provide an opportunity for the mentee to eat if you are going to be together for an extended period of time. Even if you bring a couple of sandwiches to eat together, the experience can still be rewarding.

Should you open your home? Many of the mentors who have met with my children have done so in their homes. Some have cooked or done things with their hands, and it was simply easier to do it where all their supplies were located. Some of the moms had children they couldn't leave, so my daughters met with them in their homes and saw their daily routines. This is an easier decision if you know the mentee, her family or have a good reference from others. If you do not feel comfortable opening your home, then arrange to meet at a sit-down restaurant or coffee shop with a low-key atmosphere where you can sit for 2-3 hours and chat (remember to leave a good tip!).

As I noted earlier, this is not meant to be an exhaustive list. However, these tips should at least point you in the right direction of thinking. The main goal is to head off genuine danger or potential for accusations. Use wisdom, and when in doubt, lean toward caution.

Key Points

- Review at least the first sentence of each paragraph in this chapter to consider which issues might apply to you.

12
Go and Do Likewise

While I have no conception that I have perfected the idea of mentoring, much less invented it, my passion is to see mothers and fathers, grandmothers and grandfathers, strong and mature adults of all ages to become actively engaged in mentoring. Equally, I have written books, conducted seminars and spoken to the media in order to encourage parents to recognize the need to find mentors for their children. I have spent countless hours on this because I believe that it is time for us to focus on this topic. If we give attention to it, the next generation will be better prepared for life. If we don't, then the children we did not train to make wise decisions will become our caregivers in our old age.

In writing this book, I hoped to show people how easy it can be to mentor someone for a day. By taking some of the guesswork out of it, my intent is that people would end their day of mentoring and say, "Hey! I kind of enjoyed that!" My time spent mentoring young men and women has, for the most part, always been a good experience for me and hopefully for them, too.

After the day is over, then you have a choice to make. Do you walk away from participating in the mentoring process and chalk it up as a one-off exposure to something neat or trendy? Or do you choose to become part of something bigger?

My hope is that you would take some time to reflect on what happened during your day with a mentee. Take a long hard look at the society you live in. Ask yourself if things are headed in the direction you fully endorse. Each of us have within us the ability to impact other lives, whether for good or evil. If you do not step up and make an effort to mentor the next generation in what is good, then who or what is going to be mentoring them? For too long parents and leaders have been content to let the various forms of media teach our children and youth what is true. Rather than being involved in the process, we have allowed their worldview to be shaped and formed by people whose sole interest is in making money by offering entertainment at the lowest common denominator. Or, worse, the media moguls are themselves intent on changing our society to fit their vision of a world which is not based on moral absolutes or right character.

If that seems like a bleak view, it is, I think, fairly accurate. In my lifetime, so many social mores have been obliterated. From a high-level perspective, it is clear that not only is the nuclear family under attack but so is the basic aspect of understanding one's own identity, whether in gender or even spiritual composition. This has happened during my lifetime. Truths which had been accepted and established for thousands of years across cultures and various societies have been rejected.

While it might seem easier to just fold up and lose hope, that is not what men and women of character do. Society is built on various foundational truths. Once those are destroyed, what can we do? The answer is simple: we have to rebuild those foundations. While we might not own a media company with a global reach, we have the ability to do something more far reaching. We can spend time with young men and women, with boys and girls, in order to help shape their character directly. We can engage them in conversation about the questions which come up. We can challenge the lies which are repeated over and over by the media conglomerates. By opening up and sharing our stories and our daily routines, we can reveal to them how life is lived, enjoyed and shared in the context of good and wise choices.

This is one of the reasons I have a passion to encourage mentoring. If the previous generations had done their job of mentoring us and our parents, much of what has happened in our world would have been stopped or at the least mitigated. If we choose to step up and accept our responsibility to mentor the next generation, we can prevent much of the further decay, a decay so severe that we would not even believe what is heading our way.

Your next steps are critical but also pretty simple. Identify a small list of young men or women to mentor. This could be someone who is already a coworker. It could be a group in your church. It could be one or two children at the Boys and Girls Club. Maybe it is a youth who is on a sport's team with your child. You do not have to look very far to find children who are at risk. Once you have your short list, look for or arrange opportunities to spend time together. Whether you aim for being a mentor for a day or move on to a long-term mentoring relationship, the intentional choice to act at all and mentor other people in your sphere of influence will have an overall positive influence on the rising generation.

Remember, as John Stuart Mill said long ago, "Bad men

need nothing more to compass their ends than that good men should look on and do nothing." If you want the next generation to be better than yours, make a decision to begin seeking out mentees and become a part of The Mentoring Revolution!

13
Examples of Mentoring

Although occasionally I will ask a mentor to talk about something in particular or do something in particular with my child, most of the time I give leeway to the mentor as to what he or she wishes to do. Generally, that has worked well. You may be thinking, however, "I have no idea what to do with a young person!" So I want to give an extensive list of what some of the mentors have done with my children during their mentoring meetings in order to perhaps spark some ideas of your own on how to impact a child.

Before I begin, I want to mention one thing: not everyone spent time with my children in the context of their day job. Just because a person is a dentist doesn't mean he can't go fishing with a child. If a woman is a home maker, it doesn't mean that she can't take a child for a hike. I have tried to group these by location (Work, Home and Other) in order to give some context as to how and where the mentoring took place. However, not all of the meetings stayed at one location; some were spread out over several locations.

WORK

Artist
One son learned about what goes into making themed environments. The mentor is the owner of a company which uses mostly styrofoam to create artistic and feature-

rich environments for church youth and children ministries, dentist offices, assisted living facilities and entertainment parks. My son watched as they worked on a live project, and the mentor even allowed him to help with small tasks associated with it.

Missions Director

A lady who spent time with both of my daughters had them job shadow her at her missions office. She shared with them various miracles of healing that she had experienced in her body, including a complete transformation from major deformities she had at birth. Her dynamic personality, her genuine love for people and her single-minded focus on fulfilling the Great Commission made a strong impact on my daughters.

Construction Company Owner

One son spent a day with a Ukrainian owner of a construction company. This particular day, they were building a barn for a neighbor. My son was mostly involved in handing out tools and fasteners; but the overall experience allowed him to see what goes into constructing a barn, and he got to see how quickly that type of structure can be put together when a crew works efficiently. Because the barn is not very far from where we live, whenever he passed it, it was a reminder of what he did that day.

Years later, another son spent a day with this same construction owner, who spent time talking about how he got started in carpentry. He then took my son around the city and showed him different houses and developments he had overseen. After lunch, he let my son work with his crew on the demolition of an attic in preparation for adding more living space. Because of this particular son's love for carpentry, this hands-on experience really excited him about being able to use his skills in a real-world job setting.

Special Education

A woman who works in special education had my daughter spend the day with her. She gave my daughter a good introduction to the children who were in her program and helped her understand the challenges they face. My daughter also learned more about how to interact with special needs children on their level without feeling awkward.

Mother of Triplets

A woman who has adult triplets let my daughter spend the day shadowing her at her job. My daughter helped her on various hands-on projects. She also talked with my daughter about some of the major adjustments and struggles she had to endure throughout the pregnancy and after giving birth.

Radio Station Owner

The owner of a local Christian radio station allowed my son to shadow him and hang out at his offices. My son was able to meet several of the local personalities whose programs he had listened to on the radio. The owner also shared his own career journey with my son and gave him a copy of a book he had written about his life story.

Bakery Owner

A lady who owns a bakery taught my daughter how to do custom and exquisite cake decoration. This daughter already had a business of baking bread for a regular customer base, and spending time with this mentor allowed her to see what doing this type of work full-time would look like. Throughout their day, the lady shared stories from her life, including the challenges of losing her husband in an auto accident and how God restored health to her sons and to her. Even the story of how she started the bakery is a tale of God's direction, provision and faithfulness.

Fiber Optic Technician

From my college friends, I found a fiber optic technician who allowed my son to spend part of a day with him as he spliced hundreds of fiber optic wires in a cable. He showed my son how they cut the fiber optic wires and then prepare the ends by polishing them. He also demonstrated the use of a highly technical tool which he uses to join two tiny strands of glass together in order to service voice, video and data across pulses of light.

Charity Worker

A woman who works at a local charity spent time with both of my daughters during their respective mentoring programs. Due to job loss, sickness or various life challenges, many people in our community have trouble putting food on the table. My daughters spent time unloading pallets of food or preparing bags of canned goods to be picked up by men and women who need the basics for their families. Working with this woman helped my daughters to understand that the people who need help don't always wear worn out clothes. Sometimes they drive a car and have a collar, but they have had sudden changes which have put them on the edge of practical poverty.

Banker

A loan officer at a local credit union met with my son. One important thing he helped him accomplish was to open a basic account that day. He also talked to him about the differences between a sole proprietorship, an LLC and a corporation with respect to liabilities, benefits and taxes.

Lawyer

Good lawyers may be hard to find, but lawyers who are men of godly character are probably even fewer. One such man met with my son and allowed him to accompany him throughout his day. As the counsel for the local government, he had meetings with the mayor along with the county commission as part of his daily routine. Because the lawyer took my son along, he was able to meet leaders of our government he otherwise would likely have never met. He also was able to ask him questions about his career path which included seminary, pastoring, the legal profession and a stint as an educator.

Police Officer

A police officer met with my daughter and shared her life story. She had been involved in gang activity on the West coast, was involved in terrible relationships and had a child out of wedlock. This led to her being separated from her family. Over the course of time and with help from God and her own mentors, she was able to turn her life around. Now, she is able to help people in her own community through her position with the local police force.

Chiropractor

A chiropractor spent time with my son and allowed him

to learn about what goes into taking care of the human body in relation to joints and bones. He x-rayed my son and showed him his back structure. He also related an important lesson to my son: your job will have an impact on your own body one way or another. After years of doing chiropractic work, his own body was suffering from the impact of so much pulling and jerking of other people's bodies. He had to close his practice not too long after that simply because he was unable to physically handle the work.

Executive Assistant

A lady who works as an executive assistant for a minister with a national television ministry allowed my daughter to shadow her. She talked about the challenges of keeping his schedule in order and about serving in ways that allowed him to focus on ministry while ensuring that the details got handled. As someone who had done this for years, she helped my daughter to understand more about preparing a good resume, dressing for an office environment and being organized.

Bicycle Shop Owner

The owner of a local bicycle shop met my son for a day. During that time, he watched as the owner fully assembled a customized, short-distance racing bike and then interacted with the customer who came to pick it up and try it out. He learned about different types of frames, wheels, suspensions and other parts; and he was able to spend time looking at the numerous accessories available to cyclists. The owner gave him a good understanding of what it means to be a small business owner, especially in the area of customer service. My son also contributed in a small way by cutting sheets of bumper stickers into individual units which could be given out to customers.

Public Educator

Several local school teachers have met with my daughters as part of their mentoring program. This gives my children a chance to see what public and private education look like firsthand. A teacher at a private school interviewed one of my daughters as part of her class about the novel she was in the middle of writing. She also had my daughter share with the students her experience of starting and operating a bread business to encourage them in their own entrepreneurial activities.

Office Worker

A woman in our church spent time with my daughter at her work place. During that time, she shared with my daughter the story of how she had become entangled in an affair. Instead of divorcing her, her husband chose to forgive her and to stay married to her; and their relationship is now stronger than ever. Through her testimony, this mentor helped my daughter to understand more about what unconditional love really is, both from the human perspective as well as God's perspective.

Personal Trainer

The owner of a local gym, who also serves as a personal trainer, met with my son. One of the things he taught him was the three things an athlete needs to get to the top and stay at the top: humility, gratefulness and dedication. He took my son through drills he had designed to teach balance and footwork; and because this child was involved in sports, he really enjoyed the skills he worked on that day.

Children/Youth Pastors

Our local children's pastor as well as the youth pastor spent time with my son on different days. Both of them talked to my son about what is involved in being part of such ministries. They talked about what type of work goes into the preparation for the different services they are in charge of conducting. The youth pastor even let my son watch as he prepared his sermon for that night's youth service, which he got to later listen to and enjoy.

Crisis Pregnancy Center Director

The director of a crisis pregnancy center has spent time with two of my daughters at different years. I have asked her to be open and frank about real issues. She has shared with my daughters about the real life and death issues associated with loose morals, sexual promiscuity and decisions made during dating. She also shared some of the stories of girls and women who have been disowned due to becoming pregnant outside of marriage. As someone on the front lines of the battle for the lives of the unborn, her passion for her work was contagious. Both of my daughters still place her among the top five women they each met with during their mentoring program.

Bookstore Manager

The manager of a local bookstore allowed my son to spend some time with him in a job shadow situation. Then, he introduced him to some of his employees who put him to work doing different tasks associated with shipping materials to customers or managing returns. My son got to see the grunt work associated with keeping a retail establishment filled with items. The manager also shared the story of his career journey which was filled with twists and turns.

Local Government Clerk

A lady who works in local government spent a day with my daughter going over some of the details of her job. While she is gifted with service and does her job with excellence, the effect of that day was that my daughter realized firsthand that she never wanted to have an office job like this lady's. Considering how much time and money people spend on degrees without ever knowing if they will like their jobs, I considered this to be a major win.

Newspaper Editor

A newspaper editor spent an entire shift with my son showing him what goes into producing a daily newspaper. Apart from a tour of the place, my son spent a good amount of time watching the editors at work as they prepared stories. When, on a lark, they decided to let the young kid edit a story, he found errors which they had missed. Years later, my son has noted that this was one of the first times that he began to understand that he was particularly good at writing and editing and that those are skills for which an employer or customer would be willing to pay good money.

Dance Troupe Director

The director of a Christian ballet troupe agreed to meet with one of my daughters in a city a few hours away where they were doing a performance of The Snow Queen. My daughter was able to spend time with the troupe taking classes and doing warm-ups before the show. She was able to go backstage and see what goes into producing a ballet performance at an arena. Although she only was able to spend time with the mentor mainly at mealtimes, the mentor opened up her work space and sphere of influence so that my daughter could experience a different world for that day.

Director of Marketing

The director of marketing for a large assisted living facility company let one of my daughters shadow her throughout a day. They attended meetings together and traveled to different facilities. My daughter was able to observe the lady as she listened to a water-related crisis affecting one of the facilities and as she gave instructions on how the staff were to handle it. As someone who immigrated to the United States, she also shared with my daughter some of the tough times she endured because of ethnic tension in her home country.

Widows

Several different women met with my daughters at their jobs or businesses and shared their experiences of losing their husbands through death. Some of them were very young when they were widowed. Hearing their stories of grief, tough life challenges and how they had to continue raising children or making career decisions in the midst of those times was enlightening to my daughters.

Graduate Professor

A seminary professor met with my daughter. She talked with her about pursuing higher education, getting a doctorate and teaching in a post-graduate environment. She also spent time talking about principles of prayer.

Counselor
A Christian counselor met with my daughter and talked with her about the mind. In particular, she talked about how to handle negative emotions in practical ways so that they do not control one's life. She also helped her to understand how one's thoughts can be a seed that becomes negative behavior. She taught her how to snap a simple rubber band on her wrist to help snap her thoughts back into alignment with healthy thought patterns when they start to go astray.

Financial Tips Editor
One man who operates several newsletters about financial discipline spent the day with my son. He talked with him about several aspects of the proper use of money. One of the life lessons my son learned was that living a frugal life in most areas of life allows a person to afford some large expenditures on a routine basis.

Voice Teacher
A professor in voice at a local university met with one of my daughters who loves to sing. She observed as the professor met with and taught a student. She learned some of the exercises to use in developing her own voice. The professor also shared some of the ways she has been able to use her vocal talent throughout her career and around the world.

Pharmacy Owner
The owner of a local pharmacy allowed my son to shadow him throughout the day at his business. My son participated in some hands-on tasks, such as helping sort medicines. He also learned the basics of what goes into

filling a prescription for a customer. The owner also talked to him about some good and bad business decisions he had made along the way.

Geneticist

A molecular geneticist spent part of a day with one of my daughters. As a high-level scientist, she talked with my daughter about some of the reasons she places her faith in God as the Creator rather than in evolution. In preparation for that meeting, I had my daughter contact professors, apologists and other interested parties to gather a higher-level-than-normal set of questions to cover during their time together.

Large-Scale Construction Company Owner

My son spent the day with the owners of a very large construction company. During that time, he traveled to the new airport being built in our area (one of their projects). He learned a little bit about what goes into building bridges, highways and other types of large-scale projects. He also was able to see up close some very large pieces of heavy equipment and to get a sense of their scale compared to normal automobiles.

Pastor's Wife

A lady who grew up in a pastor's home shared with my daughter about having a child out of wedlock. She was willing to not sugarcoat the difficulties she endured during this particular time of her life. In the midst of the shame she was experiencing, she met a man who was willing to marry her, treat her son as his own child and help her grow to the point that she could share a simple story of redemption with other women.

Fire Chief

The local fire chief met with one of my sons and talked to him about his career as a firefighter from the bottom up. They toured the 911 facility so that my son could learn what happens when an emergency call comes in. During the day, some of the firefighters went out on a call for a burning structure, and my son was able to hear from them about some of the dangers in answering a fire call. This structure had a few thousand rounds of live ammunition which added to the hazards of the smoke and fire. This helped my son to realize that there can be additional dangers beyond the primary emergency.

HOME

Nutritionist

One lady spent the day talking with my daughter about nutrition. Known as someone who leads a healthy, balanced life and who cooks using natural ingredients, she helped my daughter to understand the importance of putting good food into her body. She explained to her the basics of the GIGO (garbage in, garbage out) principle as it relates to the human body.

Gardener

One retired man spent time with both of my sons (different years) and taught them about gardening. One son was able to use a rototiller and actually dig up the ground. When the other son met with him, due to the weather, they were not able to plow. Instead, the mentor taught my son how to read an almanac in order to determine the best times for planting different crops.

Realtor
A realtor met with one of my daughters and talked to her about how to balance her work with family and her commitment to God. Part of the time was spent at her home, where she talked while folding laundry and straightening up the house.

Years later, this same woman met with another daughter and told her how God had spoken to her and told her to quit her job as a realtor. This actually caused some tension with her spouse who was not completely sure she was hearing from God. However, just a few months later, he was offered a major promotion in another city. By her listening to God and being obedient, she was already in a position to help her family work through the move with much less stress.

Cancer Survivor
One young woman in our community met my daughter and shared her battle with breast cancer. Currently free from cancer, she is living a full life; but she was willing to share not just the physical side of her battle but also some of the emotional questions which arose during this life challenge.

Self-Growth Coach
A former high-level executive in a large corporation spent the day with my daughter talking about various topics related to personal growth. As an author and teacher, she has a number of exercises and worksheets designed to help young women work through the process of better understanding themselves and their potential. Meeting

with women like this is part of the reason my children come away with a stronger self-confidence after their mentoring program.

Welder
A retired man spent time with my son and taught him the basics of brazing and acetylene torch welding over a three-day period. He taught him how to safely work with the tools. He spent time talking about concepts, and then they worked on some basic welding and brazing projects to give my son practical experience.

Photographer
A professional photographer spent time with one of my daughters doing a photoshoot of her. Then she allowed my daughter to use a number of props around her home to create her own still life photos and experiment with her own creativity. This particular daughter has a gift in the area of photography, and this day helped to solidify some of her interest in the subject.

Deliverance Minister
A woman who has had significant experience in dealing with the supernatural talked with my daughters about some of the encounters she has had with demon-possessed persons. She has also had numerous dreams and visions, some of which she has tied into her art (painting, textile and other). Each of my daughters left her home with a canvas which she had painted in the past, a memento of their time with her.

Salsa Cook
One lady spent time with my daughter at her home and

taught her how to make homemade salsa. They worked together preparing all the ingredients, and then they cooked the ingredients until the salsa was to their liking. She then taught her how to put the salsa into canning jars, give them a hot bath and verify that they had sealed correctly.

Retired Missionary
A retired Christian missionary spent time with my son at his farm. They fished together, and he taught my son how to make a rabbit trap. He also shared about his experiences growing up as a child from a very poor family and how his career led him to visit over 140 countries.

Prayer Warrior
One woman spent time with my daughter going over the principles of prayer. Known as a woman of prayer, she shared what she had learned so that my daughter could enjoy prayer at an early age.

Baker
One lady taught my daughter how to make a cherry pie from scratch. My daughter had fun learning how to do the lattice work with the dough on the top of the pie. After baking it, they talked about lessons of life over fresh cherry pie which my daughter had helped make.

Retired Football Coach
A man who had coached football for most of his career in education spent a day with my son. During their time together, he worked with my son on developing his punting and was able to give him some practical tips he could practice on his own.

International Homemaker

One woman who has spent most of her life working as a missionary shared with my daughter some of the practical tips she used to help make a house in another country a home for her children. Some of her tips included developing routines and making sure favorite toys or stuffed animals were always packed for trips. Her oversight helped to ensure that her children were able to feel at home in a variety of cultures and locations.

Missionaries

Several women who have worked as Christian missionaries in different developing countries have met with my daughters. Their unique perspectives on working with families and children in very poor places have helped my daughters to understand more about the real needs which exist in the world. As my daughters have coupled these lessons with their own times spent in other countries, they have learned to appreciate their own opportunities more while learning to be compassionate toward those who do not get to enjoy the same opportunities.

Hollywood Actress

A lady who has had success as an actress in Hollywood and New York talked to my daughter about the challenges she has faced as someone who has tried to live out her faith in the context of a raw and godless environment. As someone who is in the latter half of her life, her insights taught my daughter that fame at any level is not worth compromising your principles and that the end of godly or godless living both have defined rewards or consequences.

Pastor's Wife and Cancer Patient

One woman who was involved in Christian ministry met with my daughter and talked about some of the life transforming events she had in her life. Over the next few years, this woman battled a fatal health problem. As part of the mentoring experience with my daughter, we stood by her grave together for her interment and reflected on her life, her faith throughout the illness and the lessons she had shared with my daughter when they met. Having known her personally, I knew that she would have wanted my daughter to be there as her family both mourned and celebrated the fact that she was free from pain.

Internet Entrepreneur

A lady who is a business owner met with my daughter and talked with her about what it means to be an entrepreneur. She shared some about her business model of doing marketing for clients around the world from her own home. She helped my daughter to understand that being an entrepreneur means being flexible and finding solutions on the spur of the moment. She also encouraged my daughter to find her own unique contributions and to develop them into a business. Now, years later, my daughter has started her own business and is developing it using some of the lessons she learned from ladies like this one.

Mechanical Engineer

My son met with a mechanical engineer who works out of his home. He shared about his experiences of working in large companies, and he helped my son to understand the use of Computer Aided Design software in the development and design of common items used in everyday life — such as cellphones. My son gained a new appreciation for the amount of detail and the type of thought which goes into making common objects useful and available.

Piano Teacher

One of the women who met with both of my daughters is a piano teacher. She has taught piano in her home for many years and remains solidly booked with a waiting list. A very unique thing she did with each daughter was to work through actually writing a song during the day they each spent together. She prompted my daughters on writing the actual lyrics. Then she sat with them and worked through a melody. They then transcribed the melody onto a piece of sheet music. At the end of their day, my daughters each had sheet music of their original compositions.

Politician's Wife

The wife of a high-level U.S. government official took time to let my daughter spend the day with her. She invited her to come while she was having "Nana's Camp," a week of fun for her grandchildren. My daughter got to see how she is attempting to influence the current and future generations by intentionally building character into her grandchildren.

OTHER

Employment Skills Coach

A lady who works with women who are caught in the web of poverty and disenfranchisement allowed my daughter to attend one of the sessions she leads. My daughter listened and watched as she talked with the women about their challenges. She also learned that the women are taught real-life skills such as typing, sewing and such so that they can better position themselves for employment. The underlying lesson of the dangers of simply going through years of education without learning a marketable skill was highlighted by the plight these women face in their daily lives.

Gun Enthusiast
One man took my son out to a shooting range for some shooting practice. He covered topics related to gun safety and then showed him how to shoot a 9mm pistol. My son had the opportunity to shoot the pistol as well as an assault rifle.

World Traveler
At a family reunion, one of my daughters spent time with a great aunt. This lady talked with her about the importance of listening to advice and respecting authority. She also shared with her stories from her travels around the world.

Cliff Jumper
One of my sons spent time with a man who loves to experience life to the fullest. He took my son to a popular local river destination where there are cliffs and a rope swing. They first did a mild hike and then they jumped off cliffs into the river using the rope swing. My son had a blast. (One of his parents was less than impressed after hearing what they had done.) If you want to do this type of activity, however, you probably should clear it beforehand with the parents in order to avoid an awkward situation after the fact.

One woman took my daughter to a ballet performance of

The Nutcracker. They spent time enjoying the performance, and then they had a meal together where she shared her testimony and life experiences with my daughter.

Concert Promoter
My company has hosted the website for a local concert promoter for years. He met with my son in Knoxville the day that he brought in the Chris Tomlin/Toby Mac "Hello Tonight" tour. From 10 a.m. until well after midnight, he allowed my son to roam the premises with an "All Access" pass. My son was able to see what goes on in the preparation and set design for a concert. He talked with security guards and learned that this mentor is the only concert promoter who buys the security guards meals and treats them like human beings. My son talked with the roadies and watched them work. He even talked with one of Toby Mac's band members who ended up taking him onto their tour bus. While he spent very little time with the actual concert promoter, the fact that he provided access to this experience was his contribution to my son's growth.

When my daughter went through the program, the sister of the concert promoter allowed my daughter to spend the day with her when they brought in the Winter Jam concert tour. She gave her an overview of how she helps guide the business side of the concert. My daughter helped the volunteers who were tasked with counting the money brought in from the ticket booths as well as the money received during the offering. It was quite an experience for her to see that side of such a popular concert, and it was certainly the most money she had ever seen in one place in her life.

Conference Attendee
One lady took my daughter to a women's conference hosted by two of her colleagues. My daughter listened to different women share about how to grow in various areas of life. Because of the mentor's connection, she was able to eat at the speakers' table with the leaders. The mentor also bought her several books so that she could help my daughter understand that she should keep reading and never stop learning.

Professional Violinist
A professional violinist spent half a day with my daughter walking along the trails by a lake. She helped my daughter to understand that pursuing a dream or using one's talents on a larger stage requires effort to balance the demands of a career with the time due to one's family.

Scientist/Fisherman
A scientist took my son fishing. While he could have potentially done job shadowing, he spent the time doing something relaxing while talking about poignant aspects of growth and character development. In particular, he helped my son to understand that he did not need to strive to fit in with any crowd. He encouraged my son that it was okay to be different and told him that he should work to be content with being different. At the age of 13, this was an important lesson for him to hear before experiencing even greater levels of peer pressure in high school and beyond.

Author
A successful Christian author met with one of my daughters for a day. She took her around the city near where she

lives and talked with her about faith. They went book shopping to find some books which they committed to read together. The author later shared with me that the day really impacted her in a positive way.

Bodybuilder
One man who has worked as a personal trainer spent the day with my son biking and talking with him about how to take care of his body. At the age of 13, meeting with someone who has a robust and healthy physique can help drive home the lessons of the proper use of weights along with good nutrition.

Bookkeeper
A retired bookkeeper met with my son and talked to him about accounting and about growing up during the Depression era. I had encouraged my son to specifically ask questions about the mentor's childhood so he could hear firsthand stories about what that time was like, which would then impact his view of that time period in American history.

Shopper
One lady wanted to share the life lesson that it is important to have good, clean fun. She took my daughter on a most-of-the-day shopping trip. They went to numerous stores, and she bought my daughter several items of clothing. In between, she talked with her about enjoying life.

Hiker
One of the men who had been involved in children's ministry as a volunteer took my son on an eight-mile hike. During that time, he related how his wife had suddenly left

him after seven years of marriage. He talked openly about how being involved with the church kept him in close contact with other strong men. This forced him to keep in communication and not become a hermit in the midst of such adverse circumstances in his personal life. My son also learned to be sure to take plenty of water on a hike.

Pastor's Wife

When relatives get together, this can be a good time for mentoring. A pastor's wife who was visiting family spent time with my daughter and talked to her about service. She had a set of notes and thoughts she had actually prepared for their day together. They discussed the actions of service as well as the attitude which has to accompany those actions. My daughter told me that the lessons she learned that day really helped her in the way she began to approach even her chores at home. That's always a win.

Widowed Mother

One lady who was widowed with a young daughter met with both of my daughters (different years). She was very candid about the journey her life had taken, the struggles she had to endure as a single mom and the challenges she had raising a daughter in such difficult circumstances. When she met with my second daughter, she took her on their church bus to pick up inner city children for Wednesday night church. It was an eye opening experience for my daughter to see and hear about the types of situations these children have to endure. Both of my daughters learned a great deal from her about dealing with pain and loss and how to overcome life's toughest trials.

Hunter

A relative took my son out one weekend to learn how to safely use a hunting rifle. Then, on another weekend, he took him hunting. My son was able to shoot his first two deer during this time. He was thrilled to be able to actually bring home meat to put on the table. Historically, this has been seen as a big rite of passage for boys moving into adulthood, and it served as a similar emotional milestone for my son when this happened in his own life.

Tennis Player
A woman who plays tennis spent time with each of my daughters talking with them about beauty and self-perception. Western culture is immersed with plastic people who focus on outward beauty to the exclusion of all else. By talking about this real issue, she was able to bring balance to my daughters and help them to understand that inner beauty and personal character should rate higher than outward appearance.

Pastor
The pastor of a church which has grown from the teens to 2,000 members spent the day with my son talking about principles of growth. As someone who has been a long-term pastor, he was able to share some of the lessons he has learned about working with people and how to use other people's strengths in a large organization.

Acknowledgments

First, I would like to express my appreciation to the over 100 men and women who have been willing to participate in the mentoring program for my first three children. At the time of writing this book, my fourth child has begun his mentoring program. I cannot express enough my gratitude to these men and women who shared a day with my children in order to show what it is like to be in a certain career, to talk with them about how to face life's challenges, or just to go do something and enjoy life together.

I also appreciate the men and women of the Teaching of Teachers program in Central Africa who were a part of the first weeklong course I taught on the topic of mentoring. These pastors and teachers go to great lengths and personal sacrifice to further their own education so that they can better train the people in their countries and local churches. Your example of commitment to your calling and education over a period of six years is an encouragement to me.

Thanks to my wife and editor, Deana. No matter how well I think I write, she keeps me on the grammatically straight and narrow path. That being said, any errors or omissions are my own.

About the Author

Craig Thompson has served in various life development and leadership training both inside and outside the US including working with children, youth and adults using public speaking, drama, music and puppets.

His current focus involves mentoring and life development for the next generations. In 2010, Craig pioneered the 52 Godly Men and 52 Godly Women projects with his own children. In 2017, he launched The Mentoring Revolution, a mentoring curriculum for churches and community small groups which is designed to provide an easy-to-use framework for intergenerational training.

He is available for speaking engagements, seminars or conferences.

You may contact him at:

> PO Box 2605 / Cleveland TN 37320-2605

or:

> craig@walkwithgod.com

To support the author's work in leadership development, life training, mentoring and writing more books and curriculum, visit this URL:

> https://www.walkwithgod.com/giving

Comments

Did you benefit by reading this book? Did you have a good mentoring experience with a young person? If so, we would really like to hear from you. Depending upon volume, it may take a few days to receive a reply.

To share a comment on this book or a story about how it helped you, send us a note at: mentorforadaybook@thompsonpublishers.com.

Visit us on the Internet at:

      https://thompsonpublishers.com

where you can find more resources and quality books.

Errata

A list of corrected errata is maintained at:

https://thompsonpublishers.com/mentorforaday

The publisher requests that any additional errata be sent via the form on that page.

These are the companion volumes in The Mentoring Revolution Series. Do you want to help change the upcoming generations? Help get these books in the hands of parents and youth. Discounts are available for groups and bulk quantities.

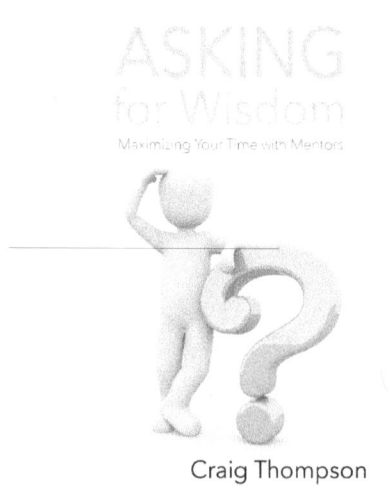

www.ingramcontent.com/pod-product-compliance
Lightning Source LLC
Chambersburg PA
CBHW052106070526
44584CB00017B/2363